APPLIED-HR:
Sense & Simplicity

205 Practical Ideas & Principles on People Management

K THIVEANATHAN

PARTRIDGE

Copyright © 2023 by K Thiveanathan.

ISBN:	Hardcover	978-1-5437-7339-2
	Softcover	978-1-5437-7338-5
	eBook	978-1-5437-7337-8

All rights reserved. No part of this book may be used or reproduced by any means, graphic, electronic, or mechanical, including photocopying, recording, taping or by any information storage retrieval system without the written permission of the author except in the case of brief quotations embodied in critical articles and reviews.

Because of the dynamic nature of the Internet, any web addresses or links contained in this book may have changed since publication and may no longer be valid. The views expressed in this work are solely those of the author and do not necessarily reflect the views of the publisher, and the publisher hereby disclaims any responsibility for them.

Print information available on the last page.

To order additional copies of this book, contact
Toll Free +65 3165 7531 (Singapore)
Toll Free +60 3 3099 4412 (Malaysia)
orders.singapore@partridgepublishing.com

www.partridgepublishing.com/singapore

CONTENTS

Reviews vii
About The Author xi
Introduction xiii
Acknowledgement xvii
Applied-HR: Sense And Simplicity xix

APPLIIED HR
Employee Engagement 1
Employee Relations 15
Career and Development 31
Culture 45
Performance Management 59
Rewards and Recognition 73
Talent Acquisition 83
Leadership 93
Interpersonal Skills 107
HR for HR 121

REVIEWS

"The author brings to life, in a novel manner, his immense wealth of experience on a wide range of leadership and functional Human Resources Management subjects. The quotes prod and provoke thinking, allowing the reader to make what they want with it. Thivi's exposure in working and leading teams across different geographies and cultures lends weight to the substance of the quotes - pivotal to the contemporary Human Resources practitioner."

– Callistus Antony D'Angelus, Global Head of Employee Relations, International Rescue Committee, USA

"Few words from a person with wisdom and experience. He shows the path forward to those who are willing to listen."

– Dr. W. John Nelson, CEO, UTAC Group, Singapore

".... have known Thivi as a credible senior leader for over a decade and in this book he's distilled his 30+ yrs of experience in a pragmatic, contextual, pearls of wisdom format.... worth reading & repeating for leaders across all levels..."

– **Gaurav Sharma,**
Chief People Officer - Coca-Cola BIG (HCCB), India

"The quotes are a collection of practical ideas learned through years of work-life experience. Its simple yet profound in meaning. It deserves to be read and revisited from time to time by both beginners and experienced practitioners."

– **Sureash Kumar, HR Director, Asia & Middle East, Beckers Group, Malaysia**

"Simple practical ideas on people management. Underneath the simplicity, lies a profound message which if reflected and acted upon, can lead to a powerful transformation for a single leader or an entire organisation".

– **Azmin Hasmat, (Ex) VP Operations, Danone, Singapore / Indonesia**

"The author offers 200 easy to read ideas and principles to guide and remind people leaders who want to build a thriving work culture."

– **Ann Chen, Senior HR Director, UTAC, China**

"A treasure trove of practical ideas on people management where complex management ideas are simplified for the new managers and HR practitioners."

— **Cornelius Koh, HR Director, Asia Pacific, St. Gobain Construction Chemicals, Singapore**

"If you hold the view that human resources constitute the most crucial asset for an organization, then Applied-HR, while being easy to comprehend, has profound message and has the potential to challenge established notions in people management. This book can guide HR Professionals, managers, or corporate leaders towards creating positive results for people and business".

— **Pavit Ngansamrej, (Ex) HR Head of ThaiCom, Thailand**

"Applied-HR guides people leaders with simplified pointers for a productive and engaging workplace."

— **Eko Susilo, HR Director, UMS, Indonesia**

"Applied-HR is about practical ideas. The material can be a catalyst for thought provoking discussions in meetings, presentations, training, group discussions or workshops."

— **Gideon Lam, CEO, Shalom International Movers, Singapore**

ABOUT THE AUTHOR

K Thivenathan, or Thivi, took an early retirement in late 2019 after spending three decades of professional life in the field of human resources. He held HR leadership roles with reputable multinational companies, such as Coca-Cola, X-Fab, Eli Lilly, Epson, and Honeywell. Prior to retirement, Thivi was the global CHRO of UTAC Group in Singapore, a semiconductor manufacturer with a revenue over USD$1B and 12,000 employees globally.

During his illustrious career, Thivi has worked or done short-term assignments in Malaysia, Singapore, Australia, China, Taiwan, USA, Thailand, and Indonesia. Post retirement, he has served as a council member of Singapore's Institute of Adult Learning (Singapore University of Social Science) until early 2022.

Thivi has successfully facilitated large-scale organisational restructuring, culture transformation, and cross-border M&A initiatives. His ability to recognise pain areas of business and address them with simple and yet award-winning people practices has won multiple industry recognitions.

Amongst the most notable recognitions are HR Leader Award (Malaysia, 2006), Best HR Leader Award Finalist (Singapore, 2011), and Asia's Best HR Team Award for Change Management (HRM Asia, 2017).

In the mid-2010s, Thivi was a member of distinguished judging panel of Aon Hewitt Best Employer Award in Indonesia and Singapore. In 2019, he was appointed to Human Resources' Advisory Panel (HumanResourcesOnline, Singapore). And, in 2023, Thivi was appointed as a member of judging panel of The HR Star Award (Chief of Staff Asia).

Over the years, Thivi has also written and contributed to numerous articles for HR magazines in the region. He has established himself as a trusted advisor and expert in his field.

Thivi is based in Singapore, enjoys spending time with extended family members and friends in Malaysia and with children in Australia. During free time, he enjoys reading, practicing yoga, and playing golf whilst keeping an eye on his investments in several start-ups.

Thivi holds a Degree in Economics from National University of Malaysia; MBA from Charles Sturt University, Australia; Diploma in Industrial Relations (ILO/MEF); and a certified Occupational Safety Trainer (AlliedSignal, USA).

Thivi is a martial arts enthusiast with a 3rd Dan Black Belt in Taekwondo.

INTRODUCTION

Years ago, as a rookie in HR, I had my own struggles to learn the ropes of HR for survival. Unfortunately, or fortunately, I have never worked directly under another HR practitioner but reported directly to business leaders from early on in my career until my retirement. This unique context has pushed me to learn the ropes of HR through the school of hard knocks and without being limited by the contemporary HR dogmas of the day.

I am a curious observer and avid reader. Thus, my thought processes are shaped mostly by my reading and personal experiences whilst searching for guidance to tackle workplace challenges in managing people. My observations of people at work helped me appreciate their needs, motivation, as well as their perception on leadership, culture, and change. Similarly, the many insightful discussions I had with various business leaders helped my understanding of the business dynamics, shareholder expectations, and the ever-changing external environment that impacts the businesses.

I learnt that almost all employees come to work with the intention to be productive, to build meaningful relationships, and to be recognised and rewarded. HR's role is to create a trusting work environment, where employees feel safe and welcomed, can have the opportunity to build relevant capabilities, and be at their best whilst striving to meet business goals. And I noted most people-related challenges are resulting from HR and leadership weaknesses towards facilitating and building a trusting work culture.

Being an economist, I was in constant search for formulas and principles that are simple and yet effective in addressing these challenges whilst ensuring desired outcomes. And this does not come easy from the books I read. Most HR books I read were either academically inclined or core messages were decoded in various chapters, making it tough to capture the principles for workplace applications. At times these messages appear highly conceptual and distanced from providing practical solutions to workplace issues I faced daily.

Thus, I started to keep a notebook to capture my hard-learned lessons at the workplace about strategies, people practices, leadership, and subtle areas such as culture, values and behaviours at work. As I grew in my professional life, equipped with wisdom from the many books I read and my observations, I continually updated my writings and summarized them in easy-to-read ideas and principles that make practical sense and simple for workplace application, i.e., 'Applied-HR: Sense & Simplicity.' This exercise helped to crystallise my thinking process in understanding the workplace issue and the options to address them. While many of the lessons in Applied-HR came from pleasant experiences, many others were evidently coming from my painful moments at work.

Over the years, the notebook became a good reference point whenever I faced similar issues and situations across various industries, regions, and cultures I had managed and lived in. It also became the catalyst for several of my HR articles, various speeches, as well as towards coaching and mentoring others. The lessons and learning in *Applied-HR* were also validated by other HR practitioners I had the privilege to work with.

Each *Applied-HR* phrase has a succinct and direct message and at times may sound unconventional and thought-provoking. The lessons from *Applied-HR* maybe self-evident to some readers whilst it may evoke different perspectives to others, given their respective situation or experience.

I must agree with the Bavarian comedian Karl Valentine who said, 'Everything has been said but not yet by everyone'. Whilst I took years to carefully articulate my experiences and thoughts in *Applied-HR*, the writings and principles in this book are probably also influenced by the many books I have read and by other established wisdoms out there.

If a career is a long road trip, mine was filled with unexpected detours, potholes, and missed turns. Nevertheless, those were my best teachable moments too. My habit in capturing the lessons learnt along that journey have been the greatest investment on myself. Thus, *Applied-HR* is the culmination of my learnings from that long road trip.

I wish I had this book when I was much younger, especially during my rookie years in HR. This book could have made my learning curve shorter, less painful, more effective, enabled me to help more people along my career journey, and probably created far much happier moments for me and for those around me.

I hope the thoughts and principles shared in *Applied-HR* will be catalysts for HR practitioners, supervisors, business leaders, corporate trainers, undergraduates, and to all those who are keen to explore the subtleties in managing people and the application of HR principles at the workplace.

Thank you for choosing to read *Applied-HR*. I wish you a pleasant career road trip ahead.

ACKNOWLEDGEMENT

I would like to express my sincere gratitude to the following people, who have influenced me with their love, support, and guidance throughout my life. Their impact on me have been invaluable, and I could not have written this book without them in my life.

I learnt from my (late) dad about punctuality and work ethics; from my mom, giving and loving without expectations; from my wife Regina, accepting others as they are; from my daughter Baenita, be vulnerable to earn trust; and from my son Baenedict, about self-discipline. My sister Medlin demonstrated unshakable faith in a better future when the present seemed gloomy; my brother Sathia never failed to get up and get stronger after each fall. And I learnt not to major in minor things from Uncle Tanka.

My trusted friend and my business partner Elayppen taught me about honesty. My first boss, Mr C K Teo, a good friend and my golf nemesis, demonstrated that leadership role is not that difficult, if you know how to hire the best and allow them do their best. Segar, my jovial friend, a talented artist, and my Taekwondo disciple, for drawing some of the delightful cartoons that are featured in this book. People management can be a serious topic. It is hoped that the cartoons may bring a light hearted touch to the readers as they journey through *Applied-HR*.

This book, *Applied-HR*, might not have come to fruition without the contribution from my good friends and highly committed HR professionals: Sureash Kumar, Cornelius Koh, Yong Yun Fui, and Alexander Yap. Their time in reading the material, suggestions, and validating my thought process have been instrumental to bring this project to a completion.

Finally, I would like to express my gratitude to my readers for taking the time to engage with the thoughts and principles presented in these pages. I hope this book will provide you with a thought-provoking and enjoyable experience.

To all, I thank you.

APPLIED HR

Sense And Simplicity

APPLIED HR

Employee Engagement

APPLIED-HR: Sense & Simplicity

1. Listen with care. Those felt heard tend to stay.

2. Without consequences, even the most productive employee will become disengaged.

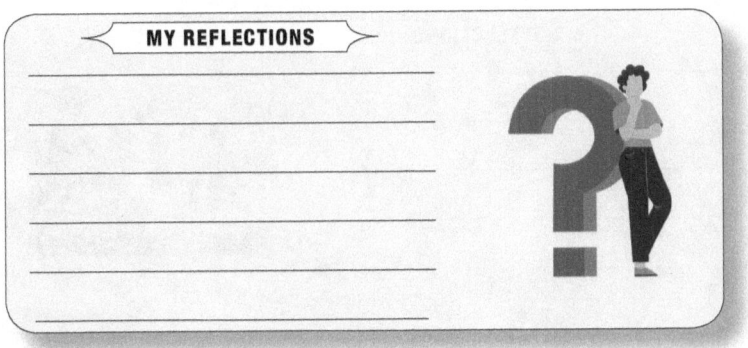

3. Inclusion is just a rhetoric if the participants are not treated as equals.

4. Recognise winners by celebrating big and small wins. Only winners will march for bigger wins.

5. Employee Engagement Score is often a lead indicator to customer engagement. Connect the dots and discern the cause and effect.

6. Most employees are self-motivated. Educate managers on how not to demotivate them.

7. The currency to buy trust is truth in words and action.

8. Engaging remote workforce demands deliberate communication processes. Capitalise the technology to maximise the socialisation.

MY REFLECTIONS

9. Most employees can handle the truth, not lies. Tell leaders to 'just be honest'.

10. A simple act of sending a 'thank-you card' makes you stand out in the crowd whilst the employee feeling over the moon.

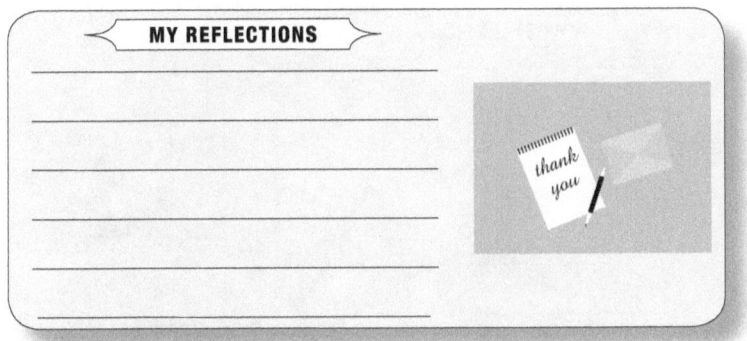

11. Policies of 'map-reading' generation have little value to the GPS-era workforce, who demands user-friendly, transparent policies, and instant answers.

12. Good employees will leave family-unfriendly workplaces more than ever before.

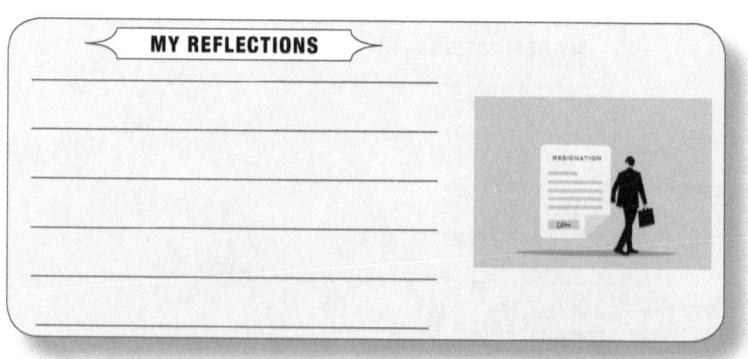

13. When faced with defensive employees, try inclusion. Seek their insights and make them feel valued. They might turn out to be your valued allies too.

14. Gaps in leadership communication are engagement derailers. Employees will fill the gap (!).

15. If you take them for granted, you will get less from them or lose them completely, including those you want to keep.

16. To truly understand employees of another generation, actively engage their contemporaries beyond those surrounding you.

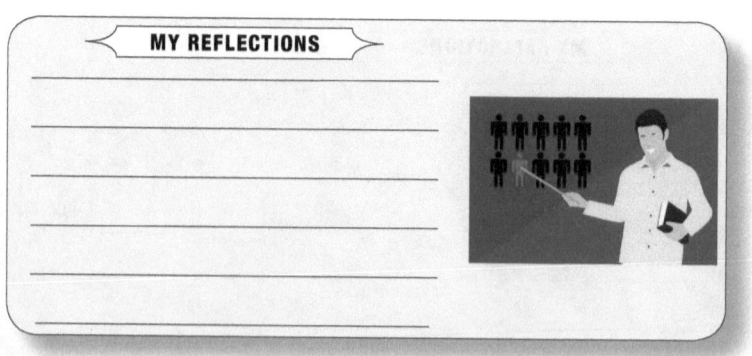

17. Seek feedback from 'Focus Groups' to help you get closer to employees' perception beyond your own intent. And it may alleviate missteps and pain.

18. A well-executed Employee Suggestion Scheme is not just an effective productivity tool but also engages employees towards a common goal.

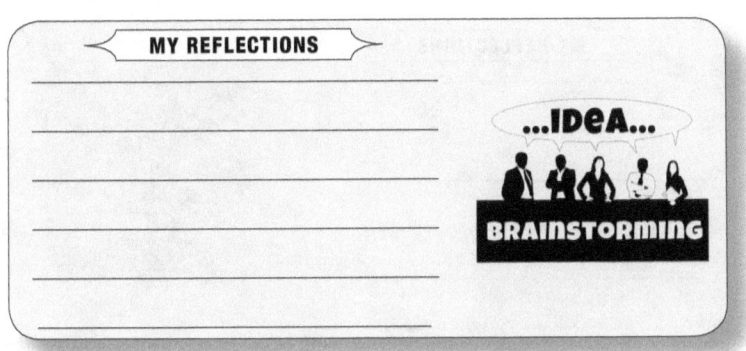

19. Dominant behaviour kills the spirit of inclusion and suppresses creativity.

20. Cross-functional on-the-job training (OJT) is probably the least expensive and yet effective intervention to build interdepartmental synergies, yet it's often underutilised.

MY REFLECTIONS

21. Design choices lead to technological outcomes, while business value choices lead to employee engagement outcomes

MY REFLECTIONS

APPLIED HR

Employee Relations

22. Lack of communication is a trust-breaker, leaving room for negative thoughts and emotions to fill in.

23. Listening is an art of try understanding the rationale of the other without filtering it with your own rationale.

24. Amongst all terminations, the most complex one is terminating for poor performance. Without a sound performance management system, it can be the most expensive one too.

25. Bad news is made worst by excuses and procrastinations. Be prompt and candid whilst highlighting the silver lining.

--- MY REFLECTIONS ---

26. Messaging is as important as the message. Pay attention to 'what' as well as 'how' you say it.

27. Routinely engage the silent majority. If not, your time and focus will be hijacked by the minority disrupters and underperformers.

MY REFLECTIONS

28. A good night's sleep is assured when you become the voice for the 'invisible'.

29. Protracted negotiation unsettles emotions. A wise leader concludes it swiftly with a win-win strategy in mind.

30. Too frequent punishments indicate a blame culture with insecurity.

31. Align managers' behaviours before addressing the union's. Union's behaviours, more often than not, are a by-product of managers' behaviours or their ignorance thereof.

32. The root cause of most accidents is unsafe act. Invest in 'behavioural safety' training for a safer workplace.

33. The hallmark of negotiation is in knowing the win even before the negotiation begins and in ensuring the other party leaves the negotiation table with a sense of winning too.

MY REFLECTIONS

34. Don't dismiss disengaged employees as 'just a few bad apples'. Work with the line managers to know them and address their concerns promptly before they become contagious.

35. Expect loyalty no more. It is transient. Embrace collaborative relationship based upon shared goals, trust, and accountabilities.

36. A disorganised union may offer a 'nuisance value' for you to take advantage of. Use it wisely.

37. When in doubt, ensure the accused gets the full 'benefit of doubt' in his defence.

38. Negotiation table is not a place to start relationship with the union but a place to capitalise your past relationships. You do not go to battleground to start a courtship.

39. Recurring employee grievances are probably signs of organisation forgetting lessons learnt from the past.

40. It is not the disgruntled employees enable unionisation but the indifferent mid-managers who perceive their own views or welfare were ignored.

41. Whilst union may bring challenging dynamics to employee relations, it does offer 'one-face' representation of all your employees with binding terms, unlike a fragmented workforce with many faces.

MY REFLECTIONS

42. Solve grievances at the lowest level possible. Escalation can break trust and may signal lack of competence.

43. Do not fret if the guilty go unpunished, but never ever let an innocent get punished.

44. Every dismissed employee deserves a fresh start elsewhere. Do your best for a soft landing.

45. You cannot keep your ears to the ground whilst in the comfort of your office. Walk around and have small talks with those on the ground. You may save painful employee relation mishaps.

MY REFLECTIONS

46. Union can be a great ally if you treat them as equals. If not, it will evolve to be a monstrous foe.

47. Develop your own workplace safety triangle. The flatter it gets, the safer is your workplace.

Note: Heinrich's Safety Triangle says 'for every 30 minor injuries, there will be one serious injury'.

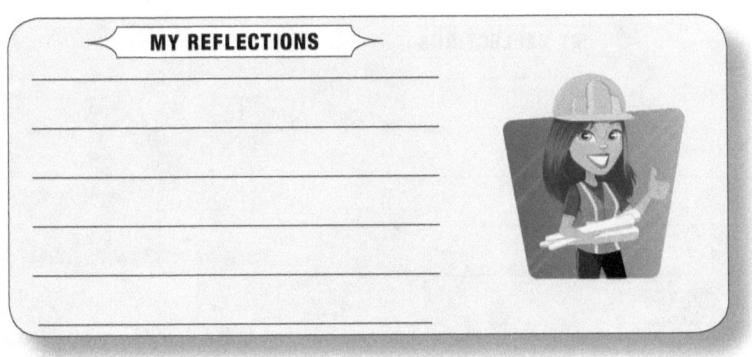

48. Every hour spent on developing employees' safe behaviours saves cost and countless hours in managing after-effects of accidents.

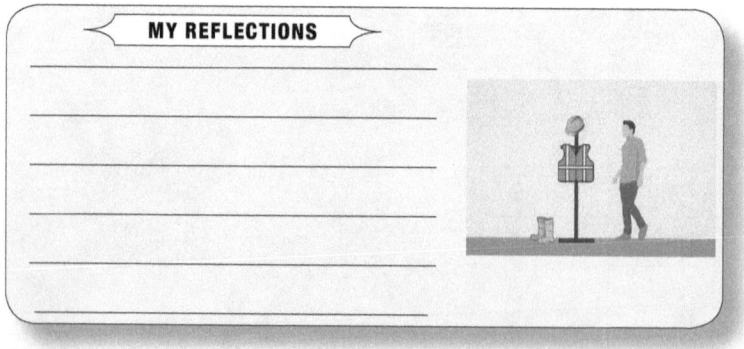

APPLIED HR

Career and Development

49. Feedback is a perception of the giver. Take it with the 'pinch of salt'.

50. There may not be one perfect mentor. Several will come and go as you are ready.

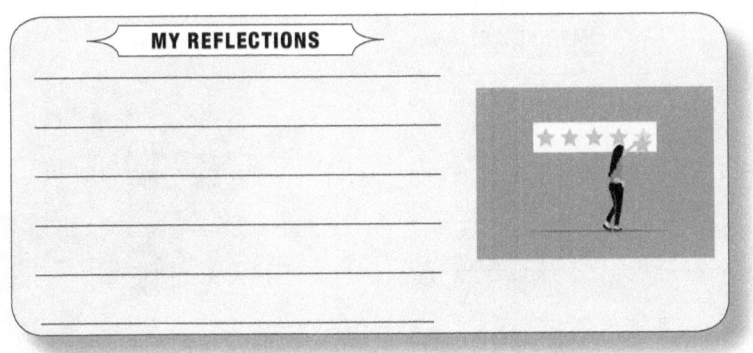

51. In accepting a mentor, you are transferring your ego to someone else whilst open to explore a better version for yourself.

52. Some jerks do get to be the bosses, especially when organisational politics get upper hand over business priorities. That is a sad truth. Your stay will then depend on how good the money is and your tolerance for nonsense.

MY REFLECTIONS

53. A panel's insights minimise individual biases and prejudices when deciding critical milestones of employee's career, e.g., promotion, performance rating, HiPo reviews.

54. Career journey is like a long road trip. Teachable moments come from those unexpected detours, missed turns, and people you meet in those moments, not from a smooth and straight journey.

MY REFLECTIONS

55. Treat each working day as if it's your first day at work. Listen more, talk less, and be a curious learner.

56. The person next to you appears luckier because he absorbed more rejection than you do.

57. If what you do makes you feel uncomfortable, you are beginning to stretch your comfort zone. If its help you get to your goals, get comfortable with uncomfortable.

58. Work on your 'Failure Resume'. It helps you face your inner fears and teaches humility.

MY REFLECTIONS

_____
_____
_____
_____
_____

59. Do not try to outshine your boss if you are career-minded. Be the enabler and create space for your boss to shine. Your boss will then take care of yours.

60. By branding the selected few as 'HiPo', the large majority are made to feel inferior.

MY REFLECTIONS

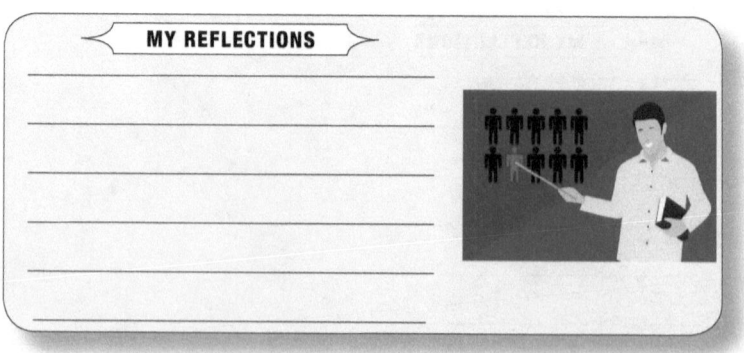

61. Those craving to learn are usually career-minded. Feed them with right opportunities.

62. Do not let line managers' turf war to short-change talents' career trajectory.

63. Your 'Failure Resume' is your real experience. Keep it in your rear-view as you move forward.

64. If you want to know what matters most for your key talents to stay, do not guess, but just ask.

Scenarios: Alex needs a good year-end bonus whilst Suresh needs flexi hours to care for his elderly parents. Jasmine feels ready for a larger role whilst Cornelius is bored and in need of new challenges. And Yong wishes for time off to finish his studies. Since no one from the company seems ready to hear them, they are exploring options elsewhere.

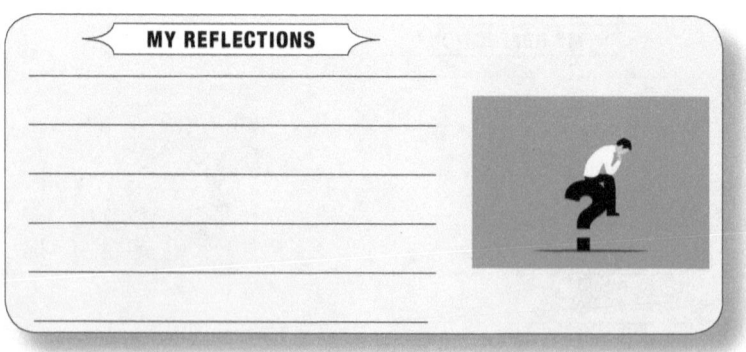

MY REFLECTIONS

65. A good talent management process includes programs to manage and develop weak performers with respect and fairness.

66. A talent-retention strategy will have 'no teeth' if it is not complemented with a career-path framework.

67. During HiPo talent reviews, focus on behavioural evidence of talents turning their positive energy to energise others. That's a mark of leadership potential.

68. If employees see career path as 'one-way up', which is usually in short supply, they will look elsewhere for growth.

MY REFLECTIONS

69. Even with a bad boss, look for the silver linings to shine. Do not be a victim but a victor until such a time to move on with heads up.

MY REFLECTIONS

APPLIED HR

Culture

70. The level of individual accountability is a direct correlation to the level of trust and transparency at workplace.

71. Grand sounding 'company values' are mere superficial statements if not articulated in supportive 'behaviours'.

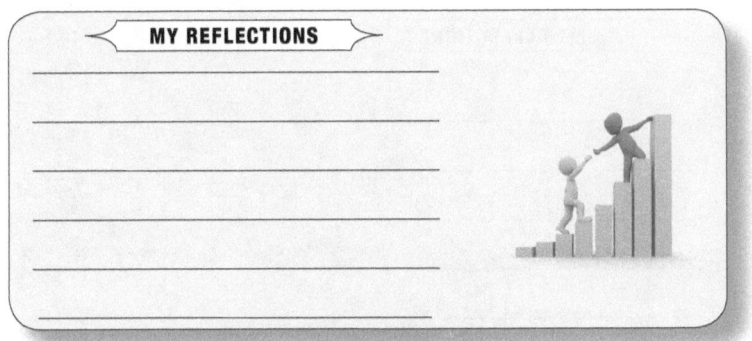

72. Processes are prerequisite for consistency, knowledge retention, and risk mitigation. If not, a culture of blame game and insecurity may set in.

73. Gossips and red tape are signs of a culture lacking trust and transparency, which eventually will erode individual accountability.

MY REFLECTIONS

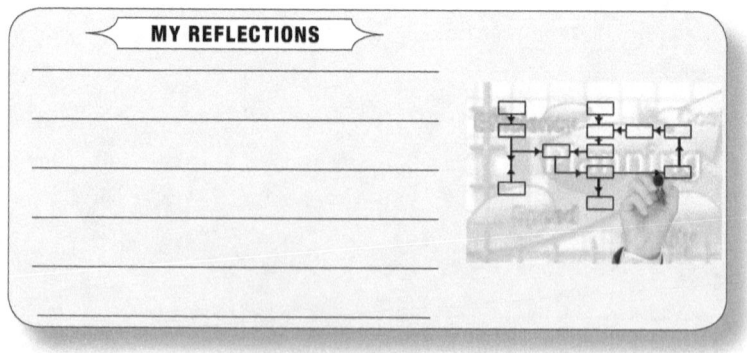

APPLIED-HR: Sense & Simplicity

74. It is not the rules but the unwritten culture that shapes behaviours at work. And leaders' behaviours shape the culture.

75. Accountability suffers when reporting line blurs.

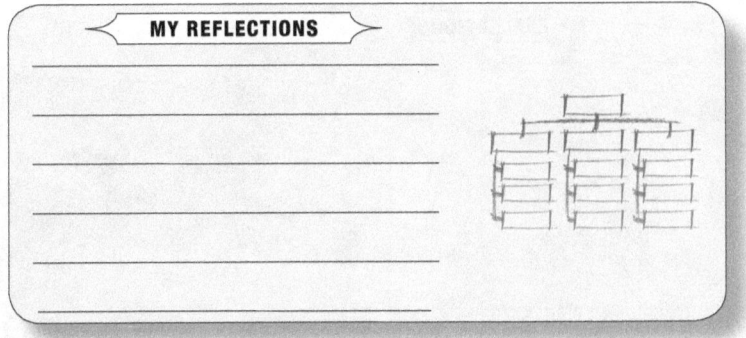
MY REFLECTIONS

76. Competitiveness and compassion are not paradoxes but complementing features of a healthy workplace. One does not need to preclude the other.

77. Organisational politics is neither good or bad. The people behind the politics matters. If it's used to advance the organisational interests, it's a healthy collaboration. If it's used to advance personal agenda, it's selfishness.

78. The real cost of protecting weak performers is the loss of high performers.

79. Informality liberates whilst bureaucracy chokes productivity and competitiveness.

Note: 'Informality' goes beyond calling your boss by first name. It's about inclusive culture ruled by mutual respect and making oneself available for candid two-way communication.

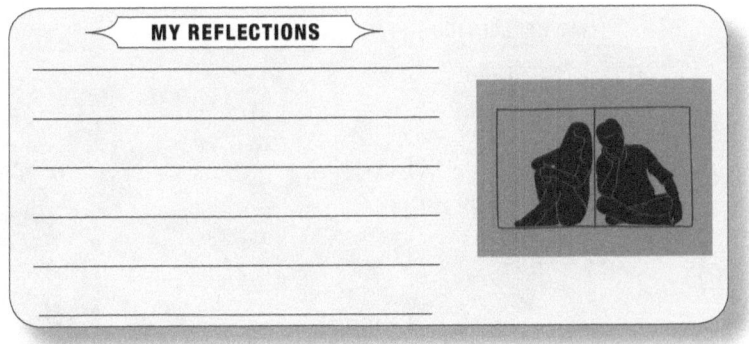

80. For positive culture-building experience, focus more on celebrating the 'role models' than punishing the delinquents.

81. Either you sell or help to sell. There is no other role in business.

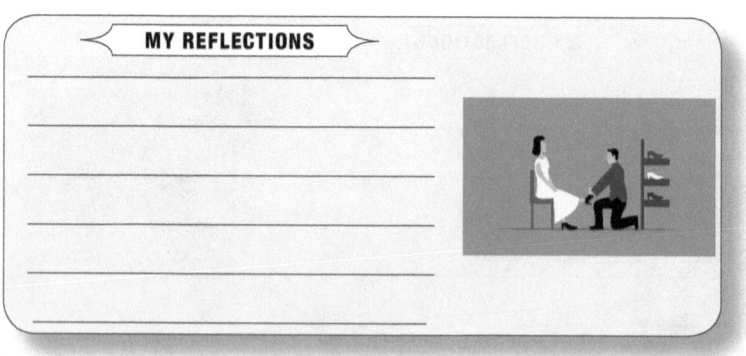

82. Exceptions are probably signs of a policy that has already run its course.

83. Onsetting of 'Peter Principle' in an organisation is as real as the conundrums related to 'Paula Principle'. Be observant.

Note: 'Peter Principle' – In a hierarchy, every employee tends to rise to his level of incompetence.
'Paula Principle' – Most women work below their level of competence.

MY REFLECTIONS

84. Fear of mistakes will overwhelm employees from trying new ideas if 'tolerance for mistakes' is not present.

85. If you shy away from publicly recognising value-driven behaviours, you will shoo away the ability to sustain a value-driven culture.

86. Even with disciplined execution, lack of follow-up and consequences can kill a high-performance culture.

87. An organisation's culture tends to reflect the behaviours of its leaders and those behaviours they tolerate.

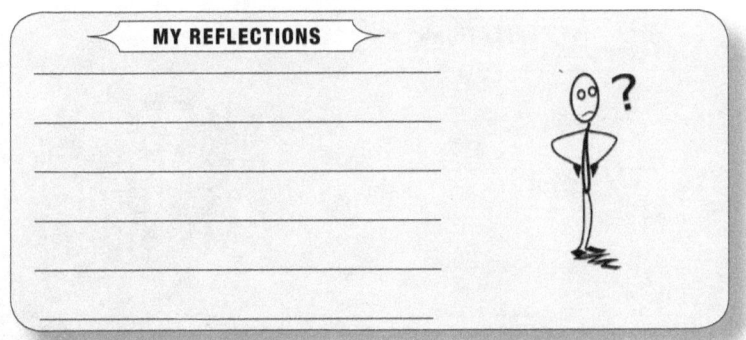

88. When brotherhood/sisterhood relationships persist beyond one's formal working life, it is a testament to a great workplace with great people.

89. If you want to avoid painful and costly accidents, get your leaders to do the scheduled safety walks and safety audits. Safety culture begins with leaders manage by walking around and reinforcing safe behaviours.

90. Employees who thrive at helping others are the sparks that shine the path for their colleagues' success. Keep an eye on these individuals to recognise and support them, to prevent them from burnout.

91. Strategy planning is an important one-off activity. Strategy implementation is a year-long activity, requiring ongoing attention and effort. When planning becomes a prolonged endeavour, businesses may paralyse.

APPLIED HR

Performance Management

92. The principle of 'equality' in treating employees does not negate HR's role in differentiating employees by merit.

93. Forced ranking encourages 'survival of the fittest'. HR is the referee ensuring the game is played fairly within rules whilst coaching the weak.

94. Performance-based pay is like making an investment. You invest more where the payback is higher.

95. 'Performance differentiation' is not something managers enjoy doing. Unfortunately, the alternative is 'mediocracy'.

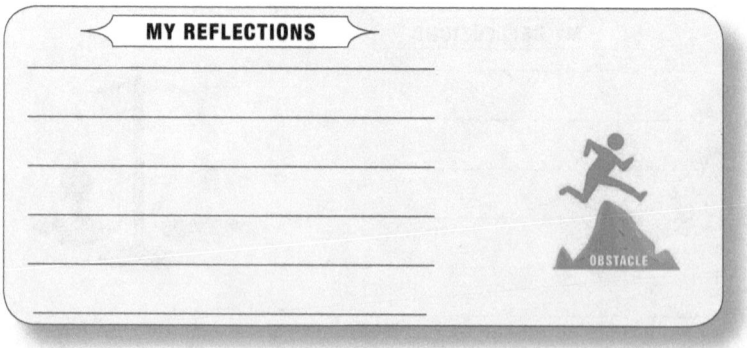

96. There is no perfect 'spans and layers' ratio. However, understanding it will provide opportunities to design right cost structure and to influence desired behaviours.

97. Majority of the bottom 10% performers are either misfit or wrong hires, not lousy employees. You have a responsibility to manage them fairly and, if necessary, facilitate a 'fresh start' elsewhere.

MY REFLECTIONS

98. A 'forced ranking process', without interventions to assist the underperformers, will appear clumsy and generate controversies.

99. Honest feedback may freak people out, but it is a blessing in disguise for those wishing to see a better version of themselves.

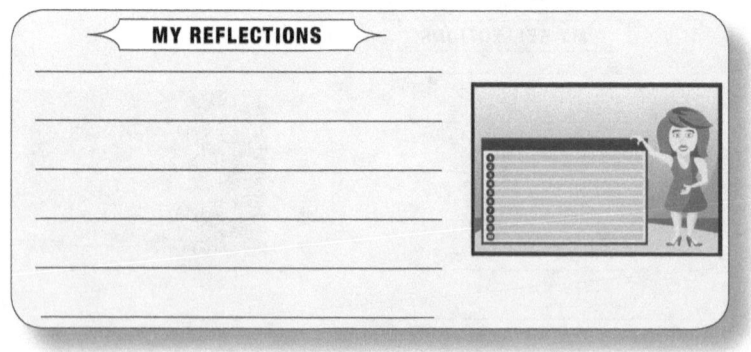

100. 'Performance differentiation', if done fairly, is akin to empowering employees to achieve their full potential.

101. Skills for 'effective performance dialogue' may sound too trivial. It is not. Never let it slip away from your training routines.

102. Excessive focus on the 'negatives' has made performance dialogue a dreaded process. Shift the weight towards strengthening the strengths for a productive performance dialogue.

103. Never end a performance dialogue without summarising the action plans.

MY REFLECTIONS

104. Without leadership commitment to performance management (PM) routines, it is just a fool's errant. It will fail to be an effective business process in aligning expectations between management and employees.

105. If a fair 'calibration process by a panel' is absent, the integrity of performance rating can be marred by individual manager's prejudices and inconsistent standards.

MY REFLECTIONS

106. Go forth and 'differentiate' employees based on performance. 'Differentiation' is the best-known method for a high-performance culture. But make sure employees know what they are differentiated for.

107. When an employee is surprised with unfavourable performance rating, the manager has failed.

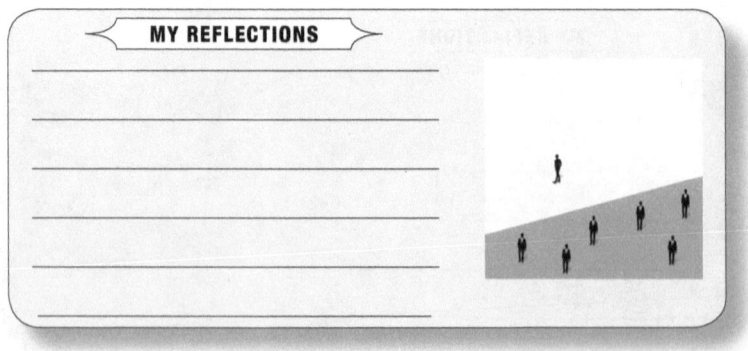

108. There is no perfect Performance Management System. Any system that helps the company hold employees accountable for their performance without surprises is a good start.

109. The rigor of your Performance Management process should withstand the intensity of scrutiny like finance audit process.

MY REFLECTIONS

110. Increasing number in poor performers is a sign of your failing rigor in Performance Management process. If not addressed promptly, valuable resources will be wasted in counterproductive measures.

111. Strengthening the strength, instead of weakness, is a more effective development intervention, provided the weakness is not a performance derailer.

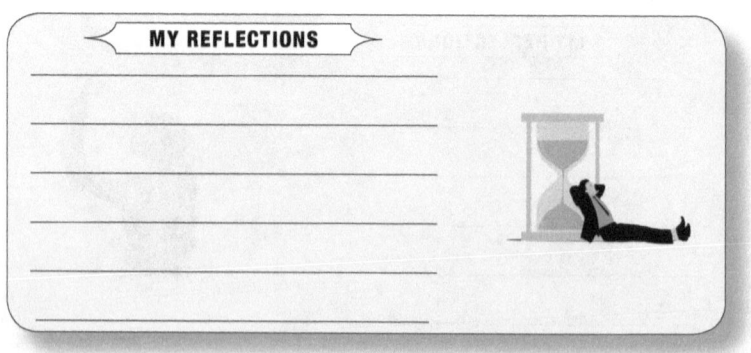

112. Performance ratings are the 'past'. Potential reviews are about the future. Do not let the past be the sole determinant of an employee's future.

113. 'More is less' when you deliver more than your past but less than what you have promised.

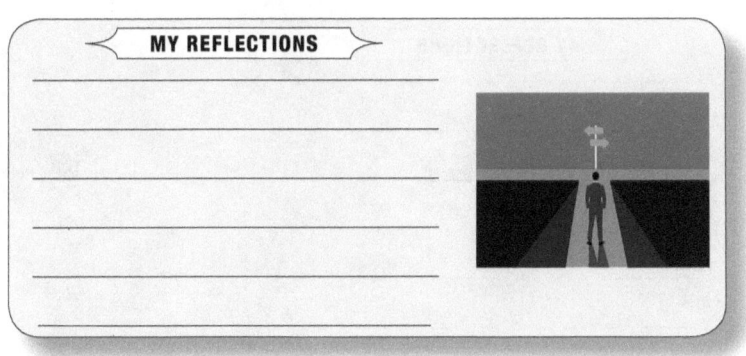

114. Without honest conversation, a high-performing culture will suffer, and being honest is not culturally sensitive but how you say it is.

115. If you are missing your performance management routines and dialogues over day-to-day operational matters, you are in the danger zone of moving away from achieving your strategic goals.

APPLIED HR

Rewards and Recognition

116. Employees will be indifferent to performance if they are unable to link pay to performance.

117. A delayed due recognition damages an employee's morale.

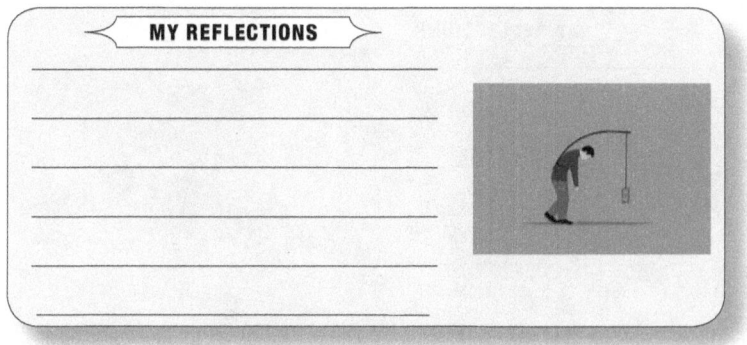

118. A 'recognition award' is more impactful if personalised, and when given amongst peers, it reinforces similar behaviours in others.

119. Reward-infused behavioural modifications are unsustainable unless it's reinforced by leadership role-modelling.

120. Indiscriminate rewards are like drugs. The recipients will expect more whilst the rest are left disappointed.

121. When reward delinked from performance, favouritism and politics will dominate the culture.

122. A merit-based reward program may unsettle employees. A good reward education program will minimise the noises.

123. For 'recognition programs' to be a culture-building block, it must be a purposeful act of celebrating right behaviours, not a mere passing reaction.

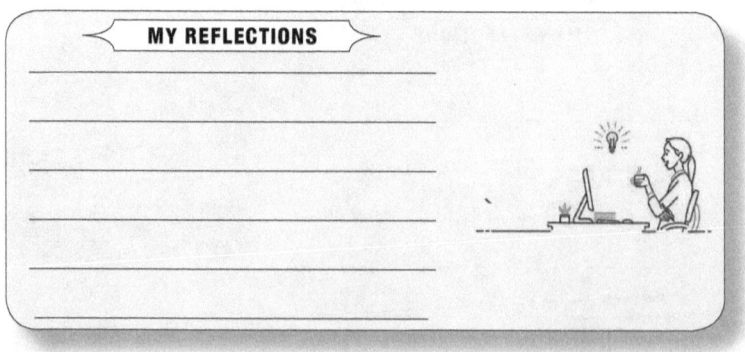

124. Influence over team performance is limited for a manager who has no authority over rewards.

125. Implementing differentiated rewards without a sound Performance Management System, which includes clear goals, candid feedback, and objective reviews, can be perceived as unfair.

126. Performance-based reward programs, if administered fairly, are 'vitamins' for the performers; 'bitter pills' for the mediocre.

127. Be the champion of celebration, big and small wins. Do not expect your boss to celebrate for you.

128. Ensure employees get what is due, regardless of the awareness on their own rights.

MY REFLECTIONS

APPLIED HR

Talent Acquisition

129. Discern candidates' high-self-confidence versus arrogance. Stay away from the latter.

130. Low job-offer acceptance rate is a red flag on your hiring process. Track it to fix it.

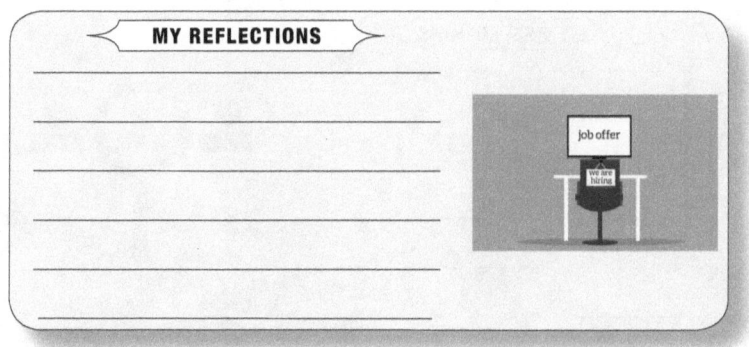

131. Regardless of the candidates' performance in interviews, treating each one with respect is a mark of your leadership quality.

132. Diversity in hiring requires conscious effort, structured approach, and candid discussion with your hiring manager. If not, the tendency is to hire your clone.

APPLIED-HR: Sense & Simplicity

133. Take risk in promoting internal candidates. They do have better success rate.

134. Each candidate walking through your reception is your brand ambassador. Do not let the untrained front-desk staff to mar your brand reputation.

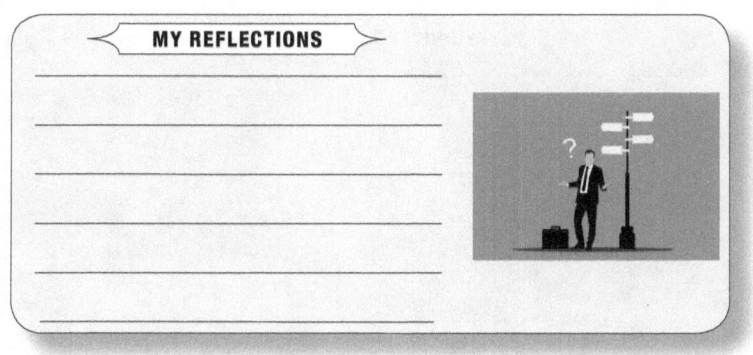

135. Ensure each interviewer has a role-specific hiring checklist (skills and behaviours). If not, hiring decision will be hijacked by unconscious biases.

136. Sadly, most formal reference checks are phony. Feedback from your own network can be the saviour from costly hiring mistakes.

MY REFLECTIONS

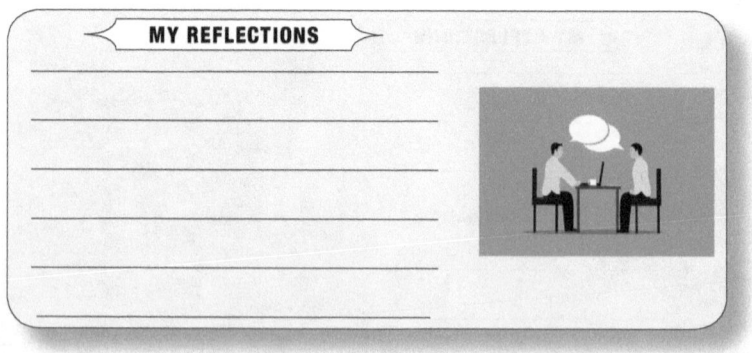

137. Each candidate you meet deserves a response. Your own reputation and company's brand image depreciate each passing day without such response.

138. If there is a wrong hire, the hiring manager got to fix it. Whilst HR is available for advice, HR is not accountable to clean up the mess.

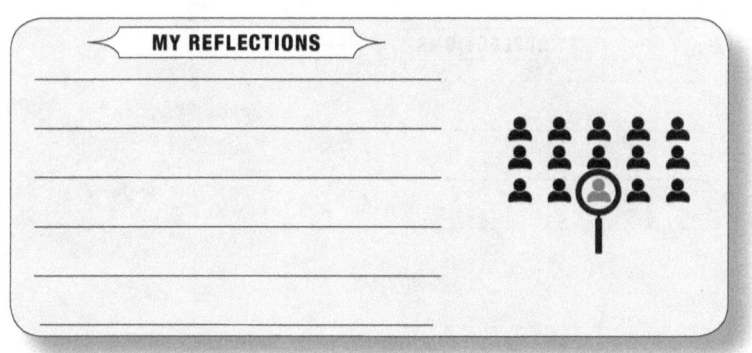

139. If you are not ten minutes early, you are late.

140. If you are surprised with a talent's exit, you have not given enough focus or time with him/her.

> **MY REFLECTIONS**
>
> _____
> _____
> _____
> _____
> _____

141. Finding a lost laptop attracts far more attention and urgency than loss of a talent. Run the $numbers$, and leaders may react differently.

142. You can reduce your hiring biases if you candidly discuss the hiring criteria with other stakeholders.

APPLIED HR

Leadership

143. If the boss misbehaved, confront him or escalate your views only if your organisation holds leaders accountable for their behaviours. Else, do not bother. Learn the 'not to do' of leadership until such a time you decide to quit, hopefully sooner.

144. Before expecting the team to march behind you, show them you care. Go beyond names to know their personal journey.

MY REFLECTIONS

145. A good leader deciphers the realities for his team and gives hope.

146. Meaningful delegation includes delegating decision-making authority whilst being available for guidance.

147. 'I took the high roads less travelled because I know my boss had my back always'.

148. When a leader is trusted, communication becomes effortless and yet effective.

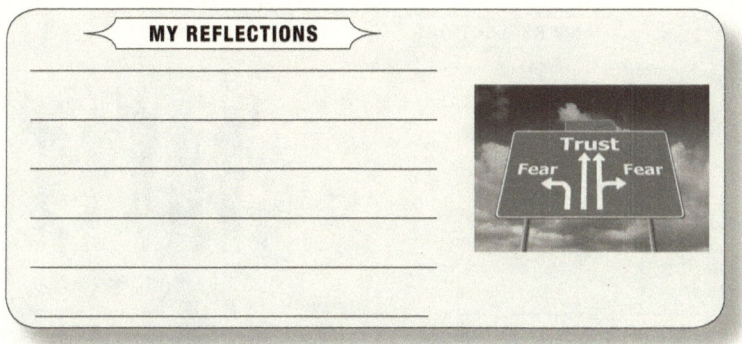

149. You are the 'CEO' of your function. Be the reason for your staff to come back to work tomorrow.

150. When integrity violation occurs, the highest-ranking officer, who is indifferent to such violation, should be 'shot' first.

MY REFLECTIONS

151. Effective leaders let their performance do the talking to earn respect. The mediocre attempts it by trumpeting their past glories.

152. When a leader disowns the team's failure, the team's trust in him dies too.

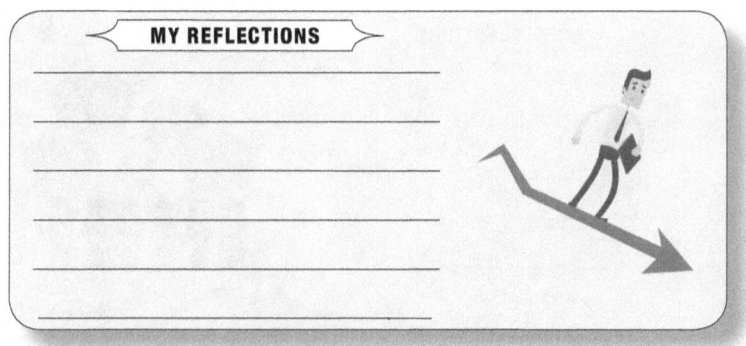

153. 'Mission' and 'value' development initiatives are leadership responsibilities. However, for 'mission', they lead from front, top-down; for 'values', they lead from behind, bottom-up.

154. Keeping harmony is an excuse of weak leaders to avoid honest feedback. A courageous leader uses feedback to unleash the potentials in employees.

155. A team is strong not because everyone is perfect but because the leader allowed each one to play to their strength for a common goal. Think of a football team!

156. Framed company values will be 'invisible' to employees without leaders' role-modelling the values.

MY REFLECTIONS

157. How you treat your lowest-level employees in their weakest moment defines your leadership values. Do it right.

158. Anyone can cheer a winning team. Only a courageous leader takes equal responsibility for a fallen team.

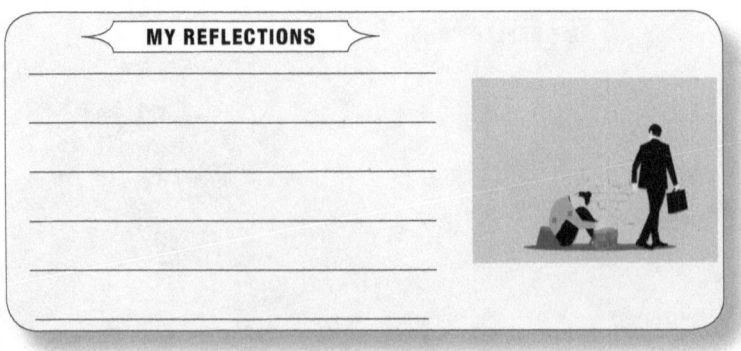

159. If 80% of ideas come from the leader, either he undermines his team's intelligence or surrounded by dummies.

160. Your skills in 'manage-down' will not ensure your team's success and recognition, unless it is complemented by your ability to 'manage-up' as well. These skills go hand in hand.

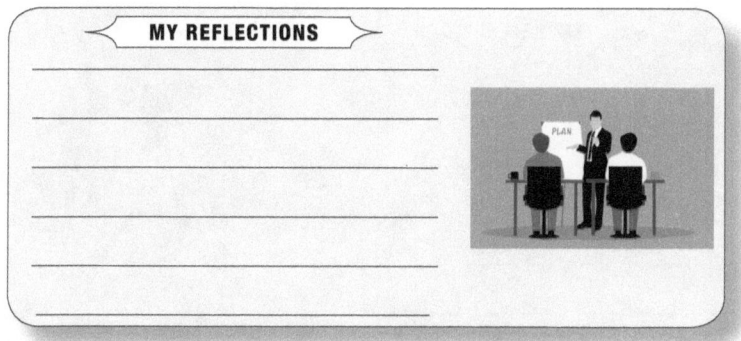

161. HR loses its strategic intent when talent and performance management processes lose the leadership attention.

162. The foremost important role of a leader is to build her best team as soon as possible. If not, she will be busy in vain troubleshooting day-to-day issues, not on the leadership role she was hired for.

163. A broad mandate reflects confidence in your team, encourages creativity, and can yield results that even surprise you.

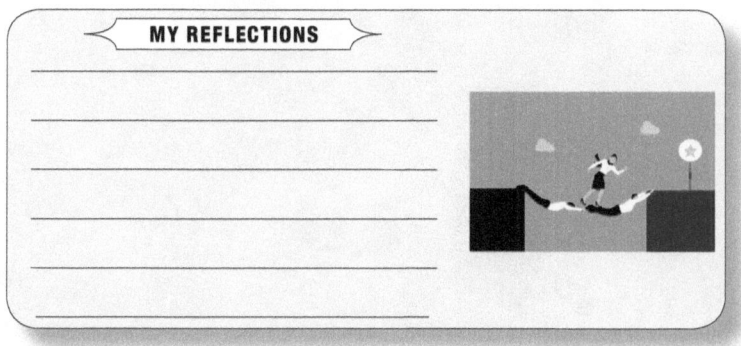

APPLIED HR

Interpersonal Skills

164. At work, be personable but impersonal.

165. In communications, being defensive can be offensive to others. Be conscious.

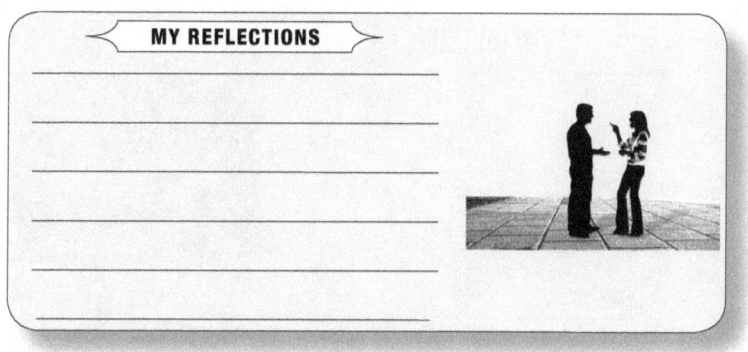

166. It's far easier to 'create happiness' than 'finding happiness', for 'creation' is within your control.

167. In arguments, if you must, remember to keep a 'door' open for the other to exit with pride.

MY REFLECTIONS

168. You are settling for less when you avoid being candid to save faces.

169. Know your battle. Avoid getting hurt fighting someone else's.

170. When in doubt, a decision to seek help from a friend, mentor, coach, or even a therapist is sign of your readiness to face your inner fears and to explore your true potentials.

171. Time management is not a common sense but a set of acquired knowledge anchored on techniques, routines, and habits.

172. If you do not like a situation or a person, you can either change your own responses or remove yourself from that situation. At times the latter is not an option.

173. Part in good terms always. Be open to the possibility that someone from your past will come handy in your future.

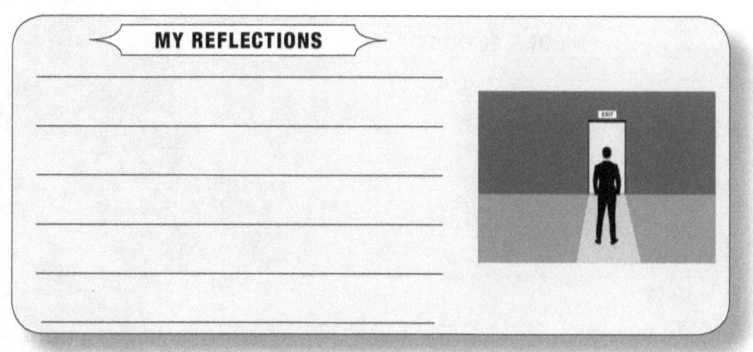

MY REFLECTIONS

174. Say 'good morning' with a smile. It boosts your self-confidence and energises those around you. It is contagious, guaranteed.

175. Whenever you hear yourself saying 'he/she doesn't understand me', consider the possibilities of you not understanding him/her.

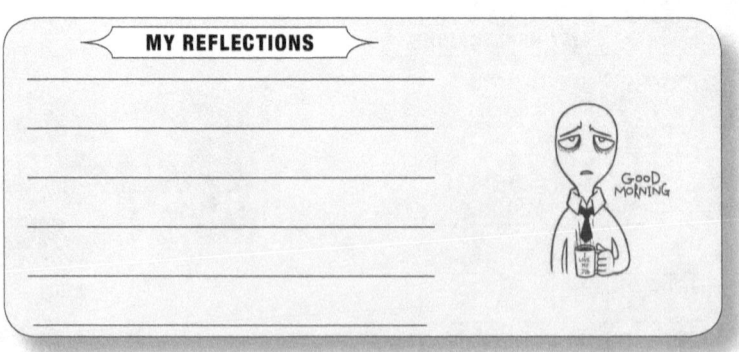

176. Avoid dictating those in different time zones to join your calls at the expense of their personal space and time. Be respectful and, if you must, take turn.

177. Whilst organising your tomorrow's calendar, be conscious not to major in minor things.

--- MY REFLECTIONS ---

178. Relationship begins through common interest/behaviour, but it thrives through complementing differences.

179. In today's culture of multitasking with conflicting priorities, listing things to 'stop doing' is equally important to your 'to do' list.

MY REFLECTIONS

180. You are a 'transient' member at work but an irreplaceable member at home. Let your life's choices reflect these.

181. Trusting and sharing are engaging whilst doubting and hoarding are harmony-wreckers.

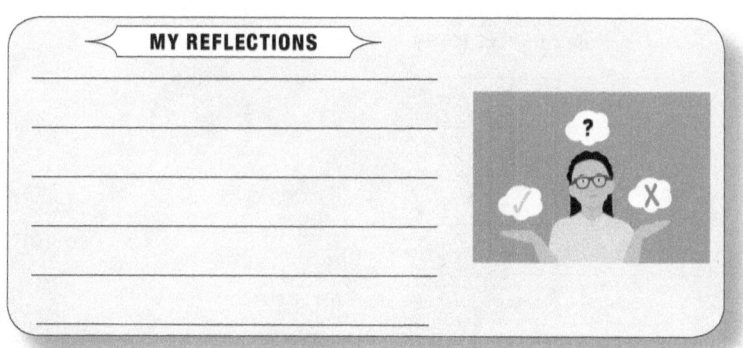

182. Apologise when feelings are hurt, and articulate your facts when the time is right. You will earn greater respect with higher moral ground, which will become handy when your chips are down.

183. If you love them, show your care on what they care about.

184. Obsessive work behaviours are not about being more disciplined. They may indicate a lack of self-awareness and/or ignorance. Whilst you may feel comfortable, it can make those around you miserable.

MY REFLECTIONS

APPLIED HR

HR for HR

185. The irony in leaders lamenting of employees lacking motivation or without competitive spirit is that their HR functions are usually under-invested and under-recognised.

186. HR is not a simple common sense or a collection of activities. It is a body of knowledge with integrated set of outcomes.

187. Story and emotions can get you attention. However, facts and numbers are needed for leadership buy-in.

188. Whilst warfare dwells in deception, HR dwells in perception, for perception is reality.

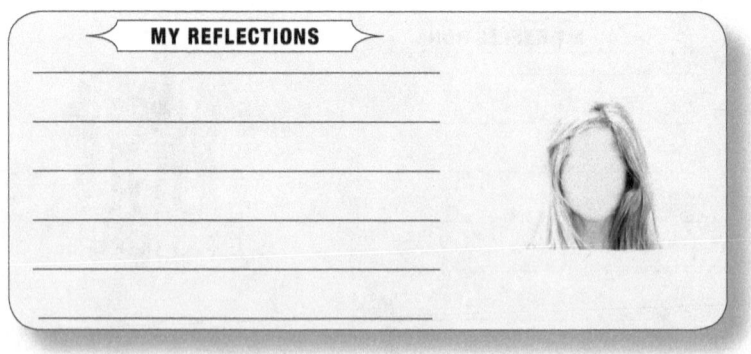

APPLIED-HR: Sense & Simplicity

189. HR's last mile is run by line managers. Make it easier for them.

190. Your HR role has the license to tell leaders what they do not like to hear. Be candid and tactful, and the right leader will respect you.

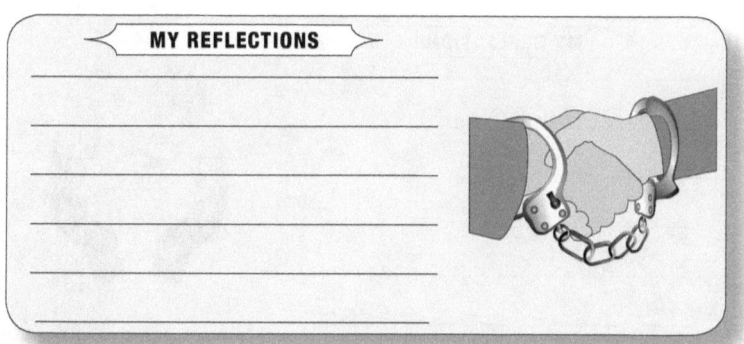
MY REFLECTIONS

191. HR is a bit of everything: It is science and art, and more importantly, it's with a heart.

192. You are an investigator, lawyer, and probably a judge too. This makes HR a delicate function, only for those with strong conscience.

193. Stand up against leaders' value transgressions promptly. It is expected of your role.

194. HR's true challenge is to build more 'flexibility' than ever before; flexibility in organizing work, remunerating employees, flexible benefits, and flexible development interventions.

MY REFLECTIONS

195. Mere objections can place HR as a 'policing' outlier. Collaborating for alternatives makes HR a sound biz partner.

196. When you ignore or cover up a leader's value transgression, it is the beginning of the end of your own leadership credibility.

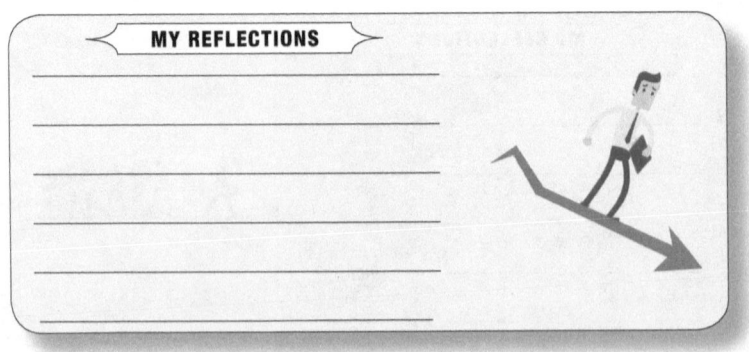

MY REFLECTIONS

197. Do not overlook HR for HR. If overlooked, it will cripple the team's ability to be the role model and change agent.

198. The line manager owns the 'firing' process as much as he owns the hiring process. HR's role is to ensure fair processes where employees' rights and dignity are not violated.

MY REFLECTIONS

199. You are the champion of communication routines. Routines build accountabilities and avoid surprises.

200. The marketing team can add the much-needed Midas touch to HR program launches. Collaborate.

201. With social media, your reputation travels faster. It precedes you wherever you go, including your next interview. Protect it.

202. If you prefer being liked more than being candid, you lose leadership credibility, trust, and respect.

MY REFLECTIONS

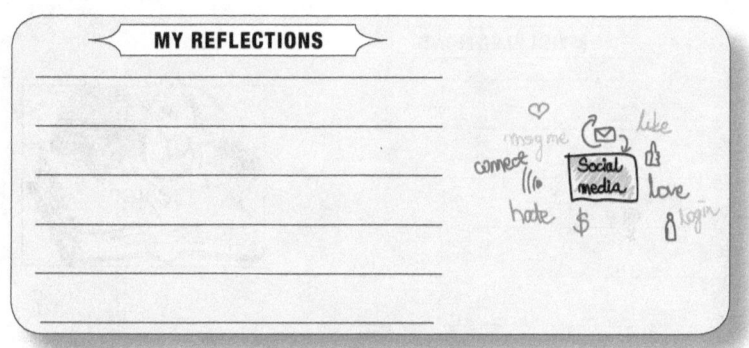

203. You have a heavier responsibility in 'communication' versus sharing information. In 'communication', you ensure the information is understood.

204. A risk-averse corporate lawyer may tell leaders to refrain from speaking their mind. Be the HRBP who coaches the leaders to be candid and honest within the legal framework.

MY REFLECTIONS

205. Work on a system and then let the system work for you. If not, you will be busy troubleshooting in vain.

www.ingramcontent.com/pod-product-compliance
Lightning Source LLC
Chambersburg PA
CBHW030750180526
45163CB00003B/973